ZERO WASTE KIDS

30 challenges to cut down waste

Kathryn Kellogg

W

FRANKLIN WATTS

LONDON • SYDNEY

Contents

What Is Zero Waste?

'Zero waste' means no waste. That's the simple answer. It means sending nothing to a landfill, a place where rubbish is buried.

But the more complex definition is to completely write waste out of existence. There are many different types of waste. You can have a waste of money, time, energy, resources, and the list goes on.

Waste is bad. It's unnecessary. It requires so much, and provides nothing in return. And we waste **A LOT**.

Did you know the average person throws out 2 kg of rubbish a DAY!? That's a lot of rubbish. Imagine if we added all of that up over the course of a year.

2 kg x 365 days = 730 kg of waste a year!

That's like 1,215 litres of ice cream or 4 full sized reindeer!

4

Waste has become a very common part of modern society, but it didn't used to be like this. If we take a trip back in time, people used what they had and they used it over and over again.

Meet Tom in 1945: Tom carries his lunch in a metal lunch box every day. Inside, you'll find an apple, an egg sandwich wrapped in an piece of wax paper that has been reused several times and a reusable flask for his tea. After lunch, Tom will carry all the containers he brought with him back home to be reused the next day.

Meet Tom in 2020: Tom carries his lunch in a plastic bag or box. Inside you'll find apple slices wrapped in a plastic packet, a turkey sandwich in a plastic sandwich bag and a small plastic bottle of water. Tom will throw away everything at the end of his meal.

Waste puts a strain on our environment. We need to step back and look at the BIG picture. Everything that we throw away had to come from somewhere first.

Everything we touch, including our rucksacks, toothbrushes, snacks and computers, is made using precious resources found on Earth, but we're using up these resources too quickly.

What Do We Waste?

Did you know there's a day on the calendar to mark when we've used ALL of the resources Earth can sustainably produce for the year?

It's called **Earth Overshoot Day** and in 2019, it was hit on 29 July. We consumed a year's worth of natural resources in 7 months. It's completely unsustainable. In fact, if everyone on Earth consumed as many resources as the average American and European, we'd need five planet Earths to sustain that way of life!

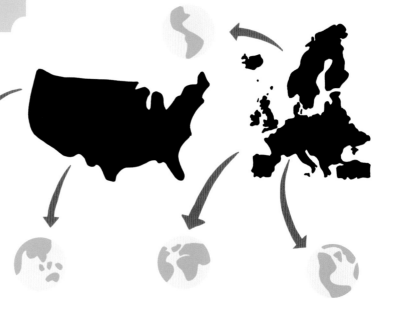

We're borrowing resources from the future at an unprecedented rate, and while this might not be a huge deal if we did it for one or two years – we've been doing it since the 1970s!

We've been living on borrowed resources for almost 50 years. We've created an ecological debt so deep that we're struggling to pay it off.

The core zero-waste challenge is to send nothing to a landfill – but it's about so much more. It's about conserving resources and protecting our natural environment.

CHALLENGE 1
Waste Audit

Do you know what you throw away on a weekly basis? What about a daily basis? What about your recycling? Do you ever think about all of the resources that go into producing those items?

Are you ready to get your hands dirty? Because it's time for a WASTE AUDIT!

What's a waste audit? It's a really fancy, professional term for going through and reviewing your rubbish. To do this, keep a log for the next week of every item that you throw away or recycle.

Keep a checklist in a notebook. After a week it might look something like this:

Juice carton IIIIII
Sandwich bag III
Chocolate wrapper II
Plastic bag II
Fizzy drink can III

The items with the most tally marks beside them are where you should start trying to make changes first.

Now, you might think that throwing away a few items isn't that big a deal, but you have to remember, you're not the only one creating rubbish – everyone else in the world is too. So when you add it up over millions and billions of people, you can see how this problem could get quickly out of hand.

'It's one straw,' said 7 billion people.

It's only one straw.

It's only one straw!

Little changes, when made repeatedly, multiplied by many people create **BIG change**! So, let's see what we can do.

Reduce - Reuse - Recycle

Now, you may be thinking that many of the items on your waste audit list like water bottles, fizzy drink cans and paper bags aren't a problem – they're recyclable!

But, unfortunately recycling presents a few more problems than you thought ...

We're often taught that recycling is THE BEST, MOST ECO-FRIENDLY thing ever. And, though it's true that recycling is great, it isn't THE best because it uses more resources and energy.

It's better to first REDUCE the amount you waste and REUSE what you can. But reduce and reuse are often skipped over because they don't make money.

RECYCLING IS THE BEST → BEST TO REDUCE AND REUSE

If you were a business and you wanted to sell a product, do you think you would have more success trying to sell it on the idea of reducing, reusing or recycling?

If you said, 'Recycling!' you'd be right. A study by Boston University, in the US, found that people were more likely to consume more if they thought the product could be recycled.

Imagine you're at a party and they're serving drinks in plastic cups. If there's a rubbish bin next to the table, people are MORE likely to use the SAME cup.

But, if you're at a party and there's a recycling bin next to the table, people are more likely to get a NEW cup.

We've been tricked into thinking that recycling will save the world, and while recycling certainly plays an important part in moving to a zero-waste world, we have to do more.

When we think about recycling, we often assume that an old plastic water bottle will become a new plastic water bottle, but that's not the way it works.

A lot of our recyclables end up in landfill. Did you know only 9 per cent of all the plastic ever created has been recycled?

We have to remember that recycling is a business, not a charity. In order for recycling to work efficiently we have to play by the rules.

This is why it's so important to recycle the right way. If we want to have our materials recycled, they need to be cleaned and sorted properly.

CHALLENGE 2
Play the Plastic Recycling Game

Learn the rules and play the game. Find out who handles your waste management. Go online to their website and work out what you can recycle.

Can you recycle plastic number 5? What about plastic number 6? Learn the rules and write them out. Put them near your rubbish bin, compost and recycling bins and make sure that each of the bins are sorted properly, and that your family is recycling correctly.

PETE or PET (polyethylene terephthalate) – COMMONLY RECYCLED – AVOID REUSING
USED IN: microwaveable food trays; salad dressing, soft drink and water bottles
IS REPURPOSED TO MAKE: carpet, furniture, new containers, polar fleece

HDPE (high-density polyethylene) – COMMONLY RECYCLED – AVOID REUSING
IS USED IN: household cleaner and shampoo bottles, milk jugs, yoghurt tubs
IS REPURPOSED TO MAKE: detergent bottles, fencing, floor tiles, pens

V or PVC (vinyl) – SOMETIMES RECYCLED – AVOID CONTACT WITH FOOD
IS USED IN: plastic pipes, shower curtains, medical tubing, cables
IS REPURPOSED TO MAKE: cables, mudflaps, panelling, roadway gutters

LDPE (low-density polyethylene) – SOMETIMES RECYCLED (check locally)
IS USED IN: cling-film, sandwich bags, squeezable bottles and plastic grocery bags
IS REPURPOSED TO MAKE: envelopes, floor tiles, bin liners

PP (polypropylene) – OCCASIONALLY RECYCLED (check locally)
IS USED IN: ketchup bottles, medicine and syrup bottles, drinking straws, carpets
IS REPURPOSED TO MAKE: battery cables, brooms, ice scrapers, rakes

PS (polystyrene) – DIFFICULT TO RECYCLE – AVOID USING
IS USED IN: disposable cups and plates, egg cartonnes, take-away containers
IS REPURPOSED TO MAKE: foam packaging, insulation, rulers

Other (miscellaneous) – DIFFICULT TO RECYCLE – AVOID USING
IS USED IN: large water bottles, CDs and DVDs, nylon, some food containers
IS REPURPOSED TO MAKE: custom-made products

One of the things that makes recycling difficult is that the rules can change from city to city, country to country. So, every time you're somewhere new, make sure that you check the rules!

10

The Challenges

As you move through this book, you will be given a set of challenges. You should have already completed two by this point! Well done!

Create a checklist of all the challenges. Stick it to your fridge or pin it up on your wall so you can track the progress you've made.

The thing about living a more sustainable life is that it's all about building small habits. Once you're in the routine of carrying a reusable water bottle or sorting your recycling correctly, you'll do it automatically.

Sustainability issues can often seem big, scary and out of your control. It's easy to feel overwhelmed and defeated.

But remember, there's **so much** you can do to help. We can fix this. If you're feeling upset about the situation, one of the best ways to curb your feelings of anxiousness is to take action. Throughout this book, you will discover simple ways in which you can use your lifestyle choices to reflect your values.

Plastic

Plastic is made from oil and natural gas. It's a product of the fossil fuel industry. It has allowed us to make some **GREAT** advancements in medicine, technology and science.

Plastic truly is a wonderful material that helps to save lives each and every day. But plastic also lasts forever. It never breaks down or goes away so every piece of plastic ever created still exists. We're using this wonderful material in entirely the wrong way.

We're using plastic for items that are in use for only a few minutes at a time. Think about it. How long do you use a water bottle for? What about a shopping bag or crisp packet?

Many of these items are only used for about 15 minutes before being thrown away.

30 mins

2 hours

5 mins

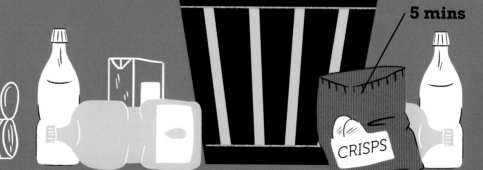

CRISPS

Let's look at the life of a toothbrush as an example.

Plastic is made from petroleum, which is extracted from the ground and can be refined to produce fuels like petrol, but it can also be refined to create plastic.

To make the toothbrush, oil is extracted from under the ground in countries such as Russia, Saudi Arabia and the US. It's shipped to a refinery in China, shaped into a toothbrush, nylon bristles are added. It's placed in packaging, then packed on a pallet wrapped in more plastic, and shipped across the world to a distribution centre.

Once the toothbrush reaches the distribution centre, it's transported to a shop where it's stocked on a shelf, from where it will eventually be picked up and brought home.

Once it's home, it's used for around three months. Then it's thrown in the bin and picked up by refuse collectors who'll bring it to the landfill where it will live ... forever.

Plastic Pollution

Sometimes plastic can escape the bin lorry and end up in waterways. So, how much plastic really makes it into the ocean?

It's a lot more than you might think. It's estimated that more than 8 million tonnes of plastic is dumped in our oceans each year.

This is a **REALLY** big problem. According to the Ellen MacArthur Foundation, a UK charity, it's expected that there will be more plastic than fish in the ocean by **2050**.

When these plastics get in the water, it becomes especially dangerous for marine life because plastic doesn't go away. Instead, it breaks up into smaller and smaller pieces.

Marine life often mistake plastic for food and they can die as a result of ingesting too much. It's estimated that 100 million marine mammals are killed each year from plastic pollution.

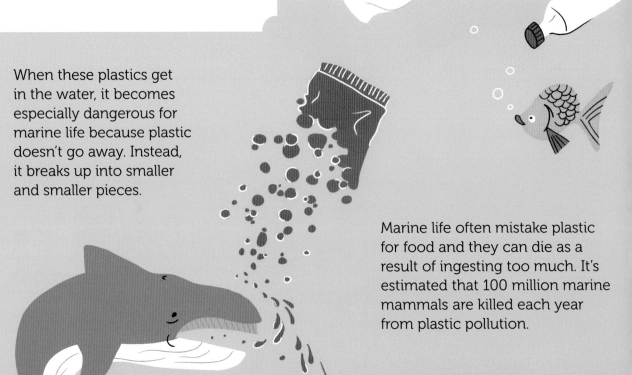

In fact, plastic can become so small that it's unable to be filtered. It becomes so, so tiny that plastic has even been found in our drinking water. According to Orb Media, a US non-profit journalism organisation, 84 per cent of drinking water worldwide (including bottled water!) is contaminated with microscopic plastic particles.

Half of all the plastic ever produced was produced in the last 13 years and it's only expected to rise.

We are in a plastic crisis! But, don't worry because you can help fix this.

CHALLENGE 3
Say NO to Straws

Let's start off easy – just say no to straws.

For most people, straws are unnecessary. They're small pieces of plastic that we don't often think about. Straws are too small to be recycled, and they're very lightweight so it's easy for them to be blown about and land in waterways.

Here's the challenge: Next time you're at a restaurant or cafe, order your drink without a straw. Go ahead and give it some practice!

I would like an orange juice without a straw, please.

CHALLENGE 4
Take It Further

Next time you go to a restaurant and see them automatically putting straws in people's drinks, find out the restaurant's email address.

Once you get home, write a very polite email, letting them know why you like going to their restaurant and asking them to implement a

STRAW ON REQUEST ONLY POLICY.

This way, straws aren't automatically handed out but only given when requested. BOOM. You just saved thousands of straws from being used!

Here's a template for you to use if you're feeling lost for words.

Good morning,

I hope you're well. (RESTAURANT) is one of my favourite places to go with my friends/family; (YOUR FAVOURITE THING TO ORDER) is my absolute favourite! During my last visit, I couldn't help but notice that straws are automatically placed in all of the drinks.

Straws and single-use plastic in general have been getting a lot of media attention recently. Straws may seem small, but they add up. Currently, 8 million tonnes of plastic end up in the ocean each year. Most of that is single-use plastic, which is responsible for killing 100 million marine animals annually.

I would like to ask that (RESTAURANT), adopt a 'straw on request only' policy. This means that straws aren't automatically put into drinks. Instead, they are only handed out when a customer specifically asks for one. This will significantly decrease the amount of straws given and have a positive effect on the environment. It will even save you money.

I really hope you'll take my request into consideration. Thank you!

Sincerely,
(YOUR NAME)

CHALLENGE 5
Bring Your Own Water Bottle

Water and fizzy drink bottles are one of the largest sources of household plastic in the ocean. People buy a million plastic bottles every single minute.

It's much better to bring a reusable bottle with you when you leave your house.

Phone, wallet, reusable water bottle, keys ...

Here's the challenge: Before you leave your house, make sure you have a reusable water bottle with you. **DON'T FORGET!**

You could start running down a checklist before you leave.

- phone
- wallet
- water bottle
- keys

This way you always have your water bottle on you. Get in the habit of carrying your bottle with you for a WHOLE month.

The Water Footprint

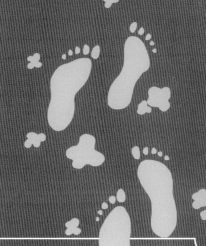

Beyond just the plastic problem, bottled water struggles with another issue – it's very water-intensive. It takes **THREE litres** of water to make **ONE litre** of bottled water! The other **two litres** are used in the creation of the plastic bottle.

Water is used to create every product we touch. It's called a **water footprint** or **virtual water**.

Many people think throwing disposable items away like paper plates, paper towels and disposable cutlery saves water because you aren't washing them. On the surface, it makes sense, right?

But, there's A LOT more to the story because we have to account for the WATER FOOTPRINT.

It takes **30 litres** of water to create **ONE** paper plate.

It takes **140 litres** of water to create **ONE** roll of toilet paper.

It takes **3 litres** of water to create **ONE** litre of bottled water.

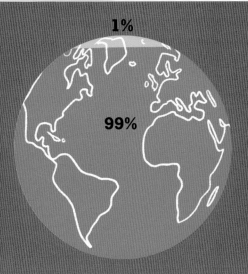

In the long run, it saves a lot of water to reuse the same item over and over again.

Water is a precious resource. According to Water.org, less than 1 per cent of the water on Earth is fresh (not sea water) and is reasonably clean and free from pollution.

That's not a lot of water – so it's really important that we conserve this resource where we can.

Reduce Your Water Consumption

In 2016, the average American home used 1,135 litres of water a day. In the UK the average household uses 450 litres per day. That's a lot of water!

You can help reduce your family's water consumption in a number of ways.

USA: 1,135 litres

UK: 450 litres

CHALLENGE 6
Save Water

Pick two new ideas to implement at home:

- Take shorter showers: time them with a stopwatch and try to beat your time every day! But make sure you've washed properly.

- Only fill the bath halfway.

- Fill up the sink to wash the dishes instead of using running water.

- Place a bucket in the shower to catch the cold water while your shower heats up. Use what's in the bucket to water your plants.

- Put out a few buckets when it rains and save the water for the garden or house plants.

- Turn off the water while brushing your teeth.

- Help your family wash fruit and veg in a large bowl instead of under running water.

Another way to save water is to opt for products without any added water. Waterless products save water, reduce packaging and cut down on overall emissions.

When you think about shipping something across the country or around the world, the more it weighs the more fuel it takes. So, the heavier an item is, the more emissions it produces.

Water weighs a lot, so when you take the water out of the product you're able to make a much more positive impact on the planet.

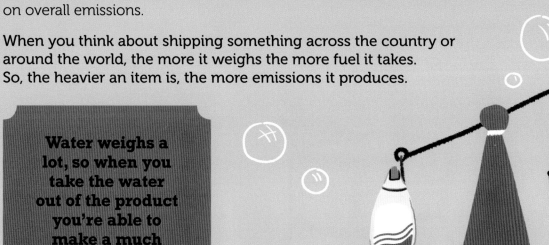

Soap

Shower gel

Here are some waterless products that are becoming more popular that you could try:

Toothpaste bits   Shampoo bars   Cleaning tablets   Mouthwash tablets

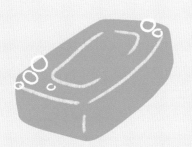

An old classic is a simple bar of soap. Before shower gel became popular, there was just soap.

Soap typically comes without packaging or wrapped in a piece of paper or a small cardboard box, it's inexpensive, and all you have to do to use it is add water.

CHALLENGE 7
Soap Is The Word

People have been worried that sharing the same bar of soap is unsanitary, but that's been proved wrong a number of times!

Make Your Own Soap

What you'll need:
· A melt-and-pour soap base
· Gloves
· A microwave-safe bowl
· A wooden spoon
· Silicone moulds
· Colour and/or herb add-ins

1. With the help of an adult, follow the instructions from your melt-and-pour base to melt the soap base. This can be done in a pan on the stove or in the microwave. **Be careful! It will be hot!!**

2. Optional: You can now add in scent and colour (see right). Add the natural colouring liquid to the soap base a small amount at a time until you have the colour you like. Add any dried herbs for scent to the base of your silicone moulds now.

3. Pour your soap base into your silicone moulds and allow the soap base to cool for 12 to 24 hours.

4. Once the soap has set, gently pull the edges of the mould away from the soap, then turn the mould upside-down and pop the soap out. It's ready for use!

To Make Natural Colours and Scents

You can make natural colourants just like making a cup of tea. With an adult's help, pour a small amount of boiling water over a few teaspoons of one of the natural products listed below. Let it sit overnight and then strain out all of the plant matter. Add this liquid to the melted soap base.

Pink: Alkanet root

Purple: Black walnut hulls

Yellow: Calendula petals, turmeric root or saffron threads

Green: Powdered parsley, rosemary or sage, spirulina or kelp powder

If you'd like to add some herbs (great for scent!), add them in the base of your silicone moulds before you pour in the soap. Great add-ins include:
• Coffee grounds
• Dried rose petals
• Dried lavender petals
• Dried rosemary
• Dried peppermint (perfect for a festive gift!)

Saving Energy

You've probably heard it a hundred times: turn the lights off when you leave the room!

Not only does that save money on the electricity bill, but you're also going to be reducing how much strain you put on the planet.

Have you ever thought about where power/energy/electricity come from?

Most of the electricity produced comes from power plants that use turbines. A turbine is a type of machine through which liquid or gas flows and turns a special wheel with blades in order to produce power. It converts energy produced by a moving flow of water, steam, gas or air into mechanical power, which is then converted into electricity.

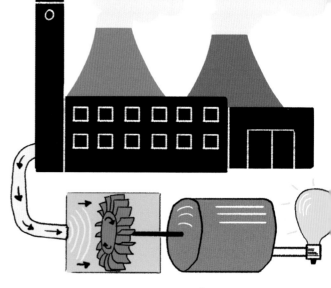

Turbine   Generator

Even devices like nuclear reactors use the same basic principle. They turn water into steam and convert it into electricity.

Think about cooking dinner over a campfire. First you'd build a fire with logs, twigs and some kindling. Then you place a big pot of water over the flames. Eventually the heat from the fire boils the water and steam is released.

Now add in a turbine and generator and BOOM, this steam is turned into energy. But any heat source can be used, it doesn't have to just be wood.

It can be:
- coal
- oil
- waste incineration
- natural gas
- peat
- biogas

This is where we run into some problems. When we burn these items, we pollute the air we breathe, which can cause serious respiratory health problems, and we release greenhouse gases into the atmosphere.

You most likely have heard of **carbon dioxide** or **CO_2**, which is a greenhouse gas. But it's not the only greenhouse gas. It's not even the most potent or strong greenhouse gas out there! It is, however, the most common one. CO_2 makes up **64 per cent** of the greenhouse gases in the atmosphere.

Greenhouse gases trap heat in the atmosphere, which is where we get the term 'global warming' from because they warm up the globe. Other greenhouse gases include **methane**, which comes from organic matter unable to break down properly in landfills and cow burps. **Chlorofluorocarbon** or **CFCs** come from aerosol cans like hairspray, cooking spray and refrigerants. **Nitrous oxide** comes from agriculture and fossil fuel industries, and fluorinated gases come from manufacturing electronics.

Fluorinated gases only make up about 1 per cent of the greenhouse gases emitted, but are one of the biggest problems. They can stay trapped in the atmosphere for thousands of years and can retain up to 23,000 times MORE heat than the same amount of CO_2.

Renewable Energy

The fastest way to prevent global warming and its disastrous effects from happening is to move from using energy created by harmful fossil fuels to using renewable energy.

Don't despair, the energy transition is already in motion. In fact, it's happening right now! Currently it is more expensive to operate an existing coal plant than it is to build a new wind farm.

Plus, there are ways you can help! You can reduce your reliance on fossil fuels in a variety of way (see pages 27–29). Here are a few types of renewable energy.

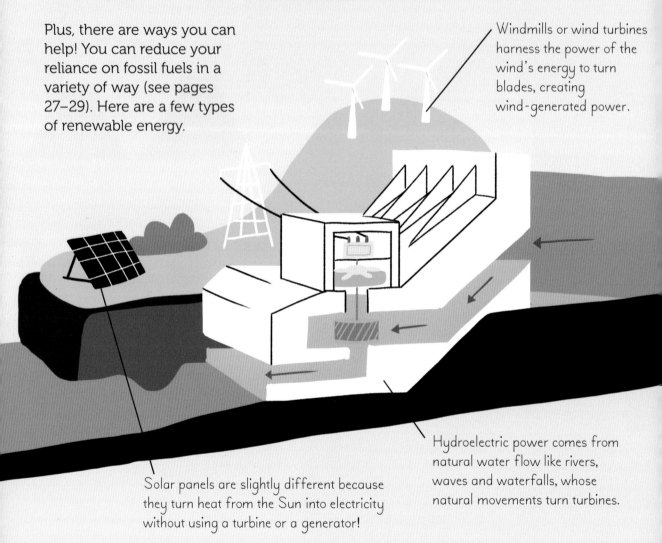

Windmills or wind turbines harness the power of the wind's energy to turn blades, creating wind-generated power.

Solar panels are slightly different because they turn heat from the Sun into electricity without using a turbine or a generator!

Hydroelectric power comes from natural water flow like rivers, waves and waterfalls, whose natural movements turn turbines.

When we use these renewable sources of energy we don't burn anything so we don't have to worry about what we're releasing into the atmosphere.

CHALLENGE 8
Energy Saving

Here are a few small ways that you can help reduce the amount of energy you consume.

1. Always turn the lights off when you leave the room.

2. When you want a snack, don't hold your refrigerator door open. Try to open it, grab what you want and shut it quickly.

3. **Unplug!** If you have your charger plugged in when it's not charging anything, it's still drawing electricity from the power grid. It's called phantom electricity – how spooky! (Also a great Halloween costume idea.)

4. Keep the temperature in your house moderate, between 18–21°C.

5. Have an electricity-free hobby. Pick up a book, draw, paint, play outside, explore!

Get Outside

Have you ever gone outside to truly marvel at how beautiful our planet is? Think about a beautiful sunset, a crystal-clear lake, a peaceful forest or a beautiful park.

There are so many beautiful sights and experiences waiting to be discovered, but often we're too busy inside watching TV, playing video games or doing homework. Going outside is important. It's key to have a first-hand relationship with what we're trying to protect and conserve.

As a bonus, going outside has been found to be incredibly helpful for improving mental health, relaxing and calming the brain.

A great way to get outside and use less energy is to walk or bike. A lot of vehicles are powered by fossil fuels so try to walk and cycle short distances instead of going by car or bus.

Walking and cycling are also great exercise!

CHALLENGE 9
Get Outside and Explore!

Instead of watching TV and playing video games, which both need electricity to work, try and spend at least 30 minutes outside each day. Here are some fun activities you can do:

- take a walk
- ride your bike
- identify native plants in your area
- find and observe five different types of insect
- pack a zero-waste picnic (see pages 48-51)
- watch for birds
- plant a small garden
- create a bee hotel
- walk or bike to a local place like school, the library or a shop
- plan a family day without vehicle travel where you walk or bike together

You can also be more eco-friendly by taking public transport or sharing cars with friends' parents!

Clothing

Clothing production is the fourth most polluting industry in the world, equal to farming livestock.

Many of the clothes we purchase in shops and online are from fast fashion retailers. Fast fashion has been designed to make you feel out of style the moment after you wear your outfit. The fashion industry has pioneered 52 micro-seasons, releasing new designs every single week to keep you coming back for more.

Back in the 1960s, the average person bought ten new pieces of clothing each year. Today, people buy around 70 new pieces of clothing each year. We're buying a lot more clothing because it's a lot cheaper than it used to be. We've managed to artificially drive costs down by sourcing cheap fabrics made from plastic, using sweatshop labour and created environmental problems like dumping toxic dyes in waterways.

Many of the people who make our clothing work in poor conditions with few safety regulations, and most aren't paid a fair wage. After all, if you're buying a £3 T-shirt, how much could the person making it actually be paid?

Beyond the human rights violations, the production is wasteful and very harmful to the environment. Producing synthetic fibres like polyester requires energy and crude oil like petroleum. Yes - polyester is plastic!

Every time you wash clothing made from synthetic fibres like polyester or acrylic, synthetic fleece made from recycled water bottles, tiny microplastic fibres are shed into our waterways. These fibres are so small that they can't be filtered out.

1 = **2,700 one litre bottle**

Even garments that use natural fibres, like cotton, use a lot of water. It takes 2,700 litres of water to make the cotton for just one T-shirt. Cotton makes up just 2.5 per cent of total cropland, but uses 16 per cent of the world's pesticides. Many of the fast fashion houses source their cotton in areas with little environmental regulations so these pesticides pollute the local area and poison the water supply.

All of this still doesn't even account for the waste side of things. According to the Ellen MacArthur Foundation: 'Every second, the equivalent of one bin lorry of textiles is landfilled or burned. An estimated US$500 billion value is lost every year due to clothing that's barely worn and rarely recycled.'

31

CHALLENGE 10
Make Do and Mend

Mend it:

Next time you lose a button on a shirt or get a hole in your jeans, don't throw them away. Repair them. With a few simple tools such as a needle and thread, they can be as good as new.

Ask your parents for help when fixing! You can always look up a YouTube video and learn a new skill together.

Upcycle it:

If your T-shirt is beyond saving, think of ways you can upcycle it. Maybe you could turn it into a cool reusable grocery bag (see pages 47–48), turn it into a T-shirt quilt or cut it into squares to use as cleaning rags or handkerchiefs!

You could also cut it into strips and make T-shirt yarn and knit or crochet something new with it.

The possibilities are endless!

CHALLENGE 11
New-To-You Clothes

Shop second-hand:
Shopping second-hand is one of the eco-friendliest things you can do for the environment.

It means no new resources have to be used to create the products you're purchasing.

Next time you want a cool pair of shoes or T-shirt, take a trip to the second-hand shop. There are a tonne of amazing and unique items you can find. It's like a mini-treasure hunt each time you go. You might also find a new toy, book or even craft supplies!

Char

Swap:
Have you ever thought about hosting a clothes swap with your friends? Invite your friends over and ask them to bring a few used (but still in good condition) items of clothing they don't wear anymore. Make some snacks like popcorn or cookies and spend the evening trying on each other's clothes. At the end of the party, everyone should have an amazing new outfit. (Make sure to check with your parents that they are happy for you to have the swap.)

In the Bathroom

Even though the bathroom is a small room, it can be responsible for a lot of waste.

Most families typically have a lot of products tucked away in cabinets, under sinks and in the shower.

Go into your bathroom, open the cabinet and count how many products your family has. Now, if you were going on an overnight school trip, how many of those would you pack?

The ones that you would pack are probably the only ones that you truly need. Of course, it's still nice to have a few that you might not use on a trip like a bath bomb or a face mask.

CHALLENGE 12
Make Your Own Face Mask

Rather than buy ready-made face masks that come in plastic packaging, why not make your own from ingredients you'll easily find in your kitchen? Make sure to ask an adult if it's ok to use them first.

Recipe:

- 2 tablespoons of mashed banana
- 1 tablespoon of pure honey
- A bowl
- A spoon

If you are allergic to either banana or honey, try yoghurt and oats.

1. Put two tablespoons of mashed banana and one tablespoon of honey in a bowl. Mix them together with a spoon to make a paste. Your face mask is ready!

2. Wash your face with warm water.

3. Pat your face dry.

4. Apply the mask with your fingers to your face, avoiding the eye area.

5. Wait 30 minutes.

 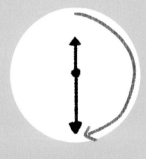

6. Rinse it off thoroughly. Your skin should feel lovely and soft.

CHALLENGE 13
A Quick Bathroom Swap Guide

Here are some items you can swap out in the bathroom.

Plastic dental floss	Silk dental floss and/or a waterflosser are great if you have dental braces.	Silk Floss
Toothpaste	Toothpowder, tooth tablets, or toothpaste in a metal tube which can be recycled.	Toothpaste
Cotton swabs/buds	You're not supposed to use these inside your ear. Instead use a flannel to clean your ears.	
Tissues	Use handkerchiefs (you can even make your own out of old T-shirts, see page 32).	
Cotton balls	Use a flannel.	
Menstrual products	Cloth pads, period panties and menstrual cups.	

One of the best ways to reduce your waste is to implement a one-in-one-out rule. So, don't get a new or different product until you've run out of an old one.

CHALLENGE 14
Toothbrush

Each year, thousands of toothbrushes are washed up on beaches across the globe. Don't let your toothbrush be a part of the problem.

We already talked about how a toothbrush is made (see page 13), but it doesn't have to be this way. Instead you can opt for one that will be composted (see pages 54–56) at the end of its life.

When it's time for a toothbrush change, switch to a compostable bamboo toothbrush. You can compost the handles, or you can also use the bodies for kindling in a barbecue. You can even upcycle them and turn them into cool craft projects.

CHALLENGE 15
Toilet Paper

In 2018, the average American used 141 rolls of toilet paper (that's 12.7 kg) per year, while the average British person uses 127 rolls or 11.4 kg. If every US household switched just one roll of regular toilet paper for a roll of 100 per cent recycled toilet paper a year, it would save 423,900 trees.

Next time you need to buy toilet paper, look for some with 100 per cent recycled content. Try to find toilet paper wrapped in paper, which can be **composted (or reused!)** instead of plastic. Even better, ask your parents about installing a bidet attachment. They're relatively cheap and will pay for themselves within a couple of months.

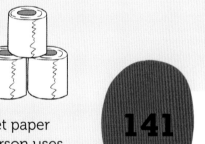

141 **USA**

127 **UK**

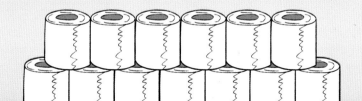

Cleaning

Who enjoys cleaning? While it's never going to be a favourite pastime, it is something that just needs doing. Having a clean space is great, but there are a lot of problems with conventional cleaning products.

Beyond their plastic bottles, their ingredients aren't very well regulated and they're responsible for a lot of indoor air pollution.

On average, indoor air pollution is two to five times worse than outdoor air quality.

It's been found that deodorants, some soaps, perfume, hairspray and household cleaning products release harmful types of pollutant that match the level of pollutants emitted by motor vehicles on the road today.

A study published in the American journal *Science* found that petroleum-based cleaning products, which can be found in many household beauty and cleaning products, emit air pollution in the form of volatile organic compounds (**VOCs**). These are the same as the ones emitted by cars.

VOCs are one of the major building blocks in creating smog, a fog mixed with air pollution caused by smoke or chemicals. Isn't it crazy to think that what's in your bathroom cabinet could be responsible for creating smog!?

Smog happens when **VOCs** interact with other particles in the air and can be responsible for health problems such as asthma, trouble breathing, heart attacks, strokes and lung cancer.

Why not just avoid the hassle and save a lot of money by making your own cleaning products?

CHALLENGE 16
Clean the Vinegar Way

Make your own all-purpose cleaner and help your family out this weekend with cleaning duties! It's easier than it sounds.

In a spray bottle, put one-part white vinegar and one-part warm water. Vinegar is an acid so it can cut through dirt, grime and grease! Give the bottle a good shake and grab a cloth cleaning rag. Spray down the kitchen table, kitchen counters, even your bathroom counter and follow up with the rag for a squeaky-clean surface! (Make sure not to get any in your eyes.)

BAKING SODA

For more difficult surfaces like the hob or bathroom sink, sprinkle some bicarbonate of soda (also known as baking soda), then spray it with your vinegar cleaner and watch it fizz and bubble up. Then wipe the surface down.

Toys and Games

The UK was one of the countries that spent the most on toys and games per child in 2017. And while the US currently has only 3 per cent of all the children in the world, it owns 40 per cent of all the toys! If you remember from earlier, zero-waste living isn't just about rubbish; it's also about resources.

When you have extra things that you don't use, you're holding onto precious resources that might be better used elsewhere. Do you have any extra toys or games that you don't play with very often? Maybe you have games that you've outgrown.

Could you give your toys or games away to someone who might use them and love them more than you do?

It can be really hard to let things go sometimes. One of the best ways to let go is to imagine someone else enjoying the items you're giving away.

CHALLENGE 17
Toy Audit

Go through all your toys and games this weekend and make several piles. Make one pile for toys that need to be repaired and then work on fixing them. Make another pile for toys and games that you can donate, but make sure they're in good condition! If your toy is completely beyond repair, you might need to throw it away. See if there are any parts that can be recycled or used to fix your other toys. Try to avoid collecting poorly-made toys like the free ones given out at events or with meals.

Also consider making a pile that you can swap with your friends. Remember the clothes swap from page 33? You can have the same sort of party with toys, board games, video games, you name it!

Remember to check with an adult before you start swapping.

THROW AWAY

DONATE

REPAIR

Food Waste

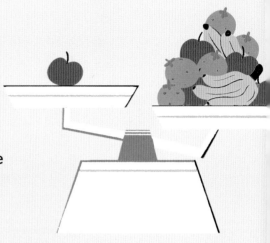

Food waste is a huge problem! According to the Food and Agriculture Organization of the United Nations, every year, roughly one third of the food produced for humans gets lost or wasted. That's approximately 1.3 billion tonnes of uneaten food! The food waste per person is between 95–115 kg a year in Europe and North America, while people in sub-Saharan Africa, south and south-eastern Asia, each throw away only 6–11 kg a year.

Food requires a lot of resources to grow and transport it. Think of all the land, water, energy and hard work it takes to grow food. It also produces greenhouse gas emissions that contribute to global warming and climate change. So we absolutely should not waste it!

Here's a few ways you can help prevent food from going to waste.

CHALLENGE 18
Waste Not, Want Not

After you finish your lunch, if you have any food leftover, put it back in your lunch box. You can eat it as a snack later. And next time you go out to eat, if you can't finish your whole meal, make sure to ask to take it away.

Instead of taking one of the disposable take-away containers, bring your own. No food waste and no packaging waste, it's a win-win! And if for some reason, you don't manage to eat it, compost it (see pages 54–57).

CHALLENGE 19
Ugly is the New Tasty

A lot of food is wasted due to quality standards that attach too much importance to the way the food looks. This happens particularly with fruit and vegetables.

So, when you're next out shopping with your family, try and find the most interesting-looking fruit and vegetables. You are sure to discover some weird and wonderful feats of nature!

Food Packaging Stats and Info

When you did the waste audit from page 7, was most of it food packaging? On average, it's in the top three most common items found in a waste audit.

We have to pay for that packaging. On average, 15 per cent of the cost of an item comes from packaging. It's pretty crazy that we pay for something just to immediately throw it away, right?

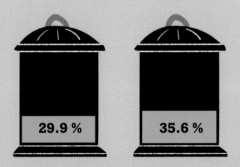

29.9 %   **35.6 %**

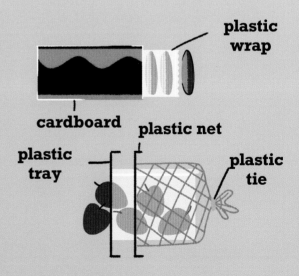

plastic wrap

cardboard

plastic net

plastic tray

plastic tie

The US Environmental Protection Agency found that containers and packaging accounted for 72.66 million tonnes of waste in 2017 in the US. That adds up 29.9 per cent of the TOTAL amount of waste created. According to Eurostat, the EU generated 88.45 million tonnes of waste in 2017, which is 35.6 per cent of the total waste created by the EU!

Thankfully there are a lot of different ways to prevent packaging waste. Let's see how!

Groceries

You probably don't make the shopping list, but you can chat with your parents about the way they buy groceries. Many of the foods that we buy are wrapped in plastic but that can be avoided in a few simple ways – see Challenge 20.

see Challenge 20.

Shopping List
Apples
Bananas
Broccoli
Cucumber
Potatoes
Pasta
Shampoo bar

The main way to have a more positive impact on the planet is to eat fewer processed foods and more whole plant-based foods. Do you remember when we talked about methane on page 25? One of the biggest sources of methane is cow burps! It also takes a lot more land, water and resources to produce animal products than it does plant-based alternatives.

methane on page 25?

For example, let's compare beef to black beans:

100 Grams	Beef	Black Beans
Protein	14 g	21 g
Water	112 l	19 l
GHG emissions	15 kg	0.56 kg
Land use	370 m^2	1 m^2

BLACK BEANS

Try and opt for more meatless meals and avoid plastic where possible. It will probably be difficult to get everything you want or need completely plastic-free/zero waste. Don't worry about it being perfect, just remember to try your best!

BURP!

FART!

CHALLENGE 20
The Hunt for Package-Free

Scope out some local supermarkets to see what you can get package-free. Any bulk bins? What about a butcher counter? Deli counter? Olive bar? Salad bar? These are all places you can get food without packaging. Make a list and ask your parents if you can help them buy some of their groceries package-free. Here are some ways to go package-free:

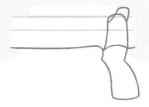

Look for loose produce rather than the produce wrapped in plastic. Bring your own cloth produce bags that can be washed and reused instead of using the single-use bags provided by the supermarket.

If you're looking to buy snacks, grains, baking supplies, and yes, even sweets, you can buy them from bulk bins. These are large tubs filled with loose ingredients completely free from packaging. You can load up in your own cloth bags or mason jars.

You can buy meat and cheese in your own containers from the butcher and deli, but try not to buy a lot of items in this area as animal agriculture is very taxing on the environment!

Avoid buying sugary drinks altogether, but if you want a treat get a recyclable can instead of a plastic bottle.

If you bring mason jars to the shop be sure to get the tare weight. This is the weight of the jar and it will be subtracted so you don't pay anything extra, only the weight of what's inside the container.

Experiment with some vegetarian dishes at home and when/if you do buy animal products, try to opt for products from local, sustainable and regenerative farms.

Farmers' Market

Another great place to find package-free food is at a farmers' market. As a society, we've got used to having different fruits and vegetables available all year round, but that's not the way it used to be.

If you wanted tomatoes and strawberries, you'd have to wait until summer. If you wanted pumpkins and apples you'd have to wait for autumn, and if you wanted peas and asparagus you'd have to wait for spring. Now, you can get those foods all year round, but they have to be flown in from all over the world.

Food can travel a long way before it gets to your plate. If you go to a farmers' market, you can actually talk to the people who grew your food, and make sure that you're getting food that is local and in season. How cool is that!

CHALLENGE 21
From Farm to Table

Locate a farmers' market near you and plan a family trip. Look at all of the beautiful and seasonal produce. Chat with the farmers about how the food is grown. If you're feeling extra adventurous buy a new or beautiful-looking fruit or vegetable and learn to make a new meal. You could also refer back to Challenge 19 on page 43 and try to find the weirdest, most unusual-looking produce!

CHALLENGE 22
DIY Reusable Shopping Bag

Plastic bags are one of the worst sources of plastic pollution. They're very difficult to recycle and not accepted in most recycling bins. Since they are so lightweight, the wind often picks them up and blows them into the environment.

Ditch plastic bags and make your own reusable bag out of one of your old T-shirts.

What you'll need:
- A cotton T-shirt (bonus points if it has a cool colour or an AWESOME design you can show the world)

- A pair of scissors

2. Fold the T-shirt in half so the sleeves line up perfectly.

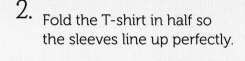

3. Cut the sleeves inside the seam (now it's a tank top!).

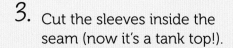

4. Open the T-shirt and cut around the neckline. You want to cut a deep U shape but not so deep that it goes past the bottom of your sleeve line.

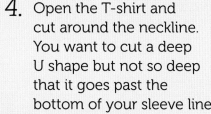

1. Turn your T-shirt inside out.

5. Make sure the bottom of the T-shirt is lined up and cut strips every 2.5 cm across the bottom about 10 cm deep.

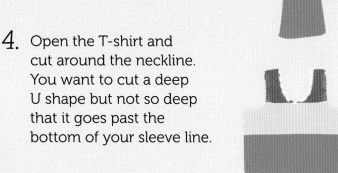

10 cm

2.5 cm

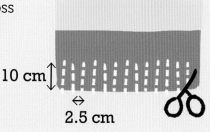

6. Tie the strips together with a tight single knot.

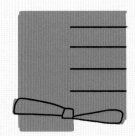

7. To strengthen the bag, tie the top strip with the bottom strip of the strip of the next pair.

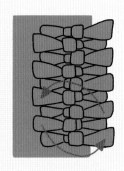

8. Double knot the end strips to reinforce them.

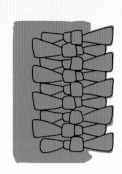

9. Flip the bag right side out and voila! You have an adorable tote bag. You can use it to carry your lunch or your clothes when you go second-hand shopping. (It would make a great present to give your friends and family too!)

Lunch and Snacks

Lunch can be the most wasteful meal of the day. Think about how many wrappers you see in the school dining hall.

If your lunches look a lot like Tom's in 2020 (see page 5) with a lot of single-use plastic, you'd be responsible for throwing away almost half a kg of rubbish for every school lunch. Throughout your time at school, that waste would be responsible for nearly ONE TONNE of rubbish. And that's just from one person! So here are a few tips for reducing your waste when it comes to packing your lunch.

CHALLENGE 23
Package-Free Packed Lunch

If you're packing a sandwich, wrap it up in a beeswax wrap (see pages 52–53), place it in a reusable metal tiffin box or wrap it in a cloth napkin.

If you're packing soup or a salad, place it in a mason jar and don't forget to bring a spoon or fork from home!

As for snacks, you can pack them in a mason jar or a reusable silicone snack bag. They work in exactly the same way as a disposable plastic bag, but can be washed and reused over and over again.

Do your parents a favour by making sure you wash your reusables when you get home so you don't add to their workload.

Even if you're unable to buy all of your groceries zero waste, try not to opt for single serving packaging. Instead opt for the larger pack and then portion it out into single serve portions yourself. Not only will this save quite a bit of packaging waste, it will also save money!

CHALLENGE 24
Package-Free Snacks

Instead of reaching for a pre-packaged snack, try your hand at making your own or opt for a snack that doesn't have a lot of packaging. Here are some ideas, and make sure to ask an adult for help if you need it!

- Seasonal fruit: oranges, apples, berries or bananas

- Snacks bought from the bulk bins like pretzels, granola, dried fruit and nuts

- Homemade trail mix: buy a small amount of a few different types of nuts and dried fruit and mix them all together.

- Veggie sticks and homemade hummus: it's so easy to make! Just blend cooked chickpeas with a little bit of water, olive oil, lemon juice, salt and pepper. Now cut up your vegetables and enjoy!

- Popcorn: you can typically buy corn kernels loose from the bulk bins. Put 50 g in a paper bag and fold the opening down a few times. Place in the microwave for 2–3 minutes. Take the bag out of the microwave and sprinkle in a bit of salt. Pour into a big bowl to eat, but save the bag to use again later.

- Apple slices and peanut butter

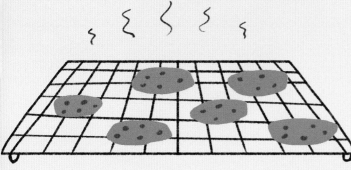

- Try making a homemade version of your favourite packaged snack like a homemade granola bar or your favourite biscuits. You're sure to find lots of recipes online.

If the weather is nice, you can use all of these tips to pack a completely zero-waste picnic.

CHALLENGE 25

Make Beeswax Wraps

A beeswax wrap is a reusable alternative to plastic food wrap or cling film. It can be composted when it reaches the end of its life. The warmth of your hands melts the wax to make it sticky.

This DIY might make a mess so ask for help or turn it into a craft night for the whole family!

What you'll need:
· Baking paper and a baking tray
· Cotton fabric with the thickness and tightness of a bed sheet. Old bed sheets or pillowcases work well (bonus points if they have a cool colour or a fun pattern). Make sure you wash them first.
· Scissors
· An oven
· Beeswax pellets
· A silicone spatula
· A coat hanger and clothes pegs

1. Ask an adult to pre-heat the oven to its lowest setting.

2. Cut your fabric to the desired size: 35 x 35 cm squares will cover bowls and sandwiches or opt for 45 x 60 cm for loaves of bread.

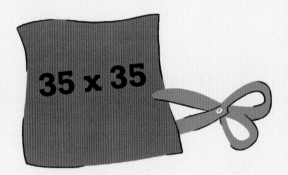

35 x 35

3. Cover the baking sheet with baking paper, lay your fabric down and sprinkle it with beeswax pellets. A small handful of pellets should be enough. Make sure to sprinkle them evenly.

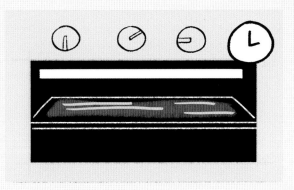

4. Put the tray in the oven and let it melt for 5–10 minutes. Keep an eye on it.

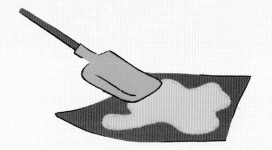

5. Once it looks like all the wax has melted, use the spatula to sweep the wax around. Ensure that all edges and corners have been covered and the wax has seeped into the fabric.

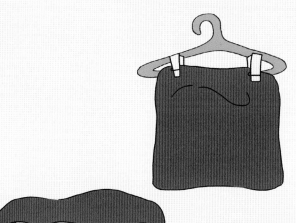

6. Wait a minute for the fabric to cool and then peel it off the baking tray, clip the wrap to the hanger and leave it to hang dry.

7. Once it's dry, it's ready to use!

TIPS!
Don't wash the beeswax wraps in the dishwasher or use really hot water. Wash them with washing-up liquid and warm water and let them air-dry.

The best way to clean beeswax off the spatula is to rinse it with boiling water.

Compost

Composting is awesome!

You might think that food scraps would break down in a landfill, but they don't. In fact, almost 60 per cent of our landfills are full of organic matter. Food waste doesn't break down because landfills were created for storage, not decomposition. So, organic matter like apple cores, peach stones, shredded paper and lemon rinds can't break down. Instead they're stuck in a state of limbo, releasing methane which is a potent greenhouse gas (see page 25).

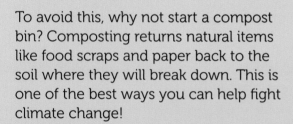

To avoid this, why not start a compost bin? Composting returns natural items like food scraps and paper back to the soil where they will break down. This is one of the best ways you can help fight climate change!

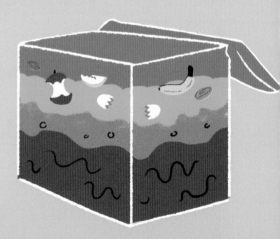

Thankfully composting is pretty easy. You can do it in your garden, in your house, through a local programme, a community or school garden, or even use a business service.

One thing to remember is that it's important to keep a good mix of carbon and nitrogen.

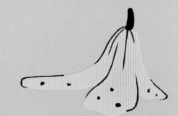

Carbon is paper, cardboard, newspaper, dry leaves, etc.

Since shredded paper can't be recycled, it's a great addition to keep your compost balanced. You can also rip up old schoolwork papers you don't need anymore.

Nitrogen is your food scraps: think coffee grounds, tea leaves, potato peel and peach stones.

What Can You Compost?

You can compost any organic material. Here are some examples:

- Ashes
- Egg cartonnes (Not styrofoam ones!)
- Bones*
- Cereal boxes
- Corncobs
- Coffee grounds
- Dairy*
- Dryer fluff
- Egg shells
- Fingernail clippings
- Fish*

- Flowers
- Fruit and veggie peels
- Grass clippings
- Hair
- Hay or straw
- Herbivore manure
- Leaves
- Meat*
- Natural fibres in small pieces: wool, cotton, linen, hemp, silk
- Newspaper

- Non-plastic tea bags
- Nutshells
- Paper bags
- Pizza boxes
- Sawdust
- Stalks
- Tea
- Toilet paper rolls
- Unbleached kitchen roll and napkins
- Unbleached tampons
- Vacuum dust

*Can only be composted in an industrial facility or a Bokashi bin (see page 56).

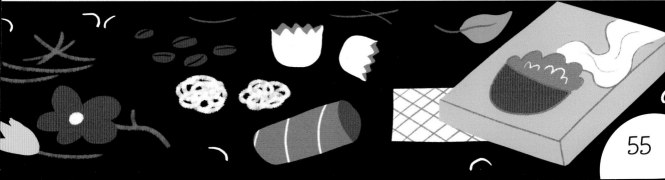

CHALLENGE 26
Where to Compost

Locate your nearest compost facility and use it. Does your school offer composting? Do you have a local community garden where you could compost? Could you use your garden or a corner of your kitchen?

Talk to your parents about the possibility of getting a compost bin set up at home and offer to take it on as one of your chores.

We throw out a lot of edible food simply because we're unsure of what to do with it.

FOOD SCRAPS
But before you take any food to your compost bin, you should ask yourself can I eat that? Many times you can!

CHALLENGE 27
Rethink Your Food Scraps and Make a New Recipe

When doing anything in the kitchen, make sure an adult is there to help.

• Strawberry tops can be infused into a delicious and refreshing flavoured water.

• Turn bruised apples into apple sauce.

• Place the roots of your green onions in a small glass of water and watch new green onions grow! You can grow lots of veggies from scraps, including garlic, ginger, carrots and even some lettuce. There are hundreds of ideas online for regrowing your food. Find one that you'd like to try this week.

Setting Up Your Compost Bin

Tumbler compost bin

There are a few different types of compost bins, but the easiest one to use for a small balcony or a garden is a tumble bin with two separate doors/chambers.

The tumble bin is very low maintenance. You just throw in your food scraps and turn the handle on the bin for proper aeration. Once one side of the tumbler is full, then start adding food scraps to the second chamber. This allows the first chamber to completely break down. Once your food waste has turned into compost, you can use it for your house plants, garden, or give it away to friends or neighbours for their next gardening project.

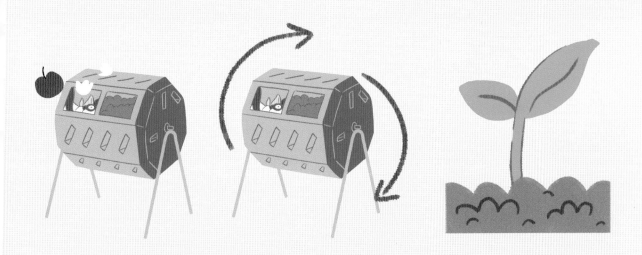

If you don't have a garden or balcony, a Bokashi bin is the perfect indoor composting bin. It uses a mixture of enzymes to break down all of your food scraps.

CHALLENGE 28
Plan a Zero-Waste Party

One way of reducing waste is to keep your party small. Instead of a big bash, invite a few close friends to participate in one of your favourite hobbies together. You could bake and decorate your birthday cake together, for example.

If you prefer a bigger bash, here are some tips for reducing waste!

Presents: Make a wish list for your friends and family and ask for experience gifts and consumable gifts instead of physical gifts.

Experience gifts are things such as tickets to go to the cinema, a gift card to your favourite ice-cream shop or a class you want to take. Consumable gifts could be a bath bomb, candle or your favourite sweets. Don't forget to specify that you either don't want presents wrapped or ask people to wrap them in newsprint so you can recycle it!

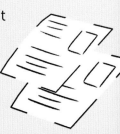

Party bags: Get small reusable cloth bags and fill them with sweets to hand out to your guests. Include a small note asking them to reuse the bags the next time they go shopping.

Keep it real: If you're having a party at home, use real dishes, real cups and cloth napkins. You can even try out different napkin-folding styles: bows, swans, fans, the possibilites are endless. A good tip is to make sure that the washing machine is empty when the party starts! After the party, throw all of the cloth napkins into the washing machine while you wash the dishes.

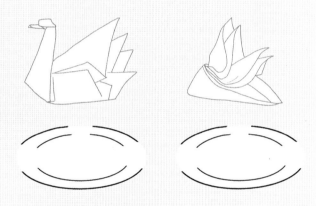

Keep it minimal: Keep your decorations minimal and compostable. The easiest way to do this is to decorate with nature! Flowers and leaves are so beautiful. It's an easy way to be fun and festive without being left with a lot of rubbish.

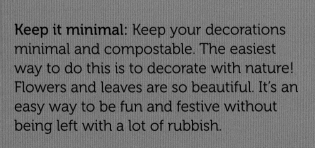

Upcycle Craft

So many great things can be made out of stuff we throw away. When you turn a waste item into a useful item it's called upcycling. Before you put anything in the recycling bin, you should ask yourself, what can I make with this?

CHALLENGE 29
From Junk to Treasure

Make a craft with something upcycled. Cardboard boxes can be turned into tiny villages or used as storage boxes. Paper printed only on one side can become a new colouring page or folded into a unique fun shape. Get creative! There are loads of fun upcycled craft ideas on Pinterest.

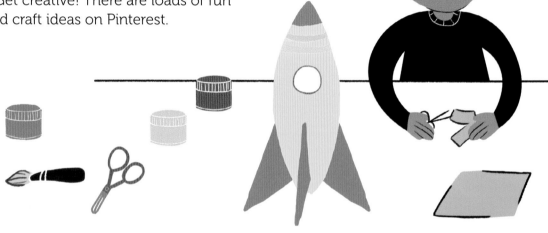

GET INVOLVED

Now that you're personally saving the world, it's time to take things one step further. One of the best ways that you can help save the world is to simply talk about it. Many people are afraid of having hard conversations and talking about the world's problems, so it's time to speak up and show your friends, family and classmates how they can get involved!

When you talk about the climate crisis, it's important to be calm and level-headed. Share your personal story. Talk about what works for you on your zero-waste journey.

CHALLENGE 30
Organise a Zero-Waste Event

Work on organising an event this year. Here are some ideas for you to get involved with your local community:

Organise a beach clean-up day if you live near a beach, or a park clean-up day, if you live near a park.

Talk with your city council about environmentally friendly projects you can take part in. Maybe propose one of your own like a plastic straw ban or styrofoam ban.

Help others learn new DIY skills.

Grow your own food or compost at a community garden.

Teach others how to buy food the zero-waste way.

Plan a zero-waste week at school.

Zero-waste living, sustainable living, saving the planet, whatever you call it, can feel pretty intimidating. After all, you're just one person. You might wonder if what you're doing will really make a difference.

It absolutely will. Through your actions, you're influencing the people around you to make better choices. So if you're ever feeling down, imagine what the world would look like if everyone believed their actions made a difference. It would look pretty amazing, right?

Most of us can do small things to have a positive impact on our environment, and it's important to remember, you don't have to be perfect! You just have to give it a try.

Glossary

aeration a process that allows air to become mixed with water, soil, etc.

atmosphere the mixture of gases around Earth

compost to collect and store plant material so it can break down and turn into soil

conserve to protect something from being wasted or destroyed

consumable possible to eat, drink, or use up completely

consume to use

contaminated poisonous or not pure

cropland land used for growing plants in large quantities such as cotton or wheat

decomposition the process of rotting

disposable made to be thrown away after use

eco-friendly not harmful to the environment

emit to produce and send out

environment the air, water and land in or on which people, animals and plants live

enzyme a chemical substance produced by living cells that causes a chemical reaction

fossil fuel a fuel, such as gas, coal and oil, that was formed underground from plant and animal remains millions of years ago

generator a machine that turns energy into electricity

greenhouse gas a gas, such as carbon dioxide, that traps heat in the atmosphere

impact a powerful effect

implement to start using a process

industry the people and activities involved in one type of business

ingest to eat or drink something

overwhelm to feel sudden strong emotion

particle an extremely small piece of something

petroleum a dark, thick oil obtained from under the ground, used to make petrol and plastic

refinery a factory where natural resources, such as oil, are made pure so they can be tranformed into something else

regenerative can be grown again

reliance the state of depending on something

renewable energy a type of energy that can be replaced and will never run out, such as energy from the Sun or wind

repurpose to find a new use for something

resource something that comes from nature, such as water and wood, which has value and can be used to create things

sustainable can be done for a long time because it doesn't damage the environment and won't run out

sweatshop a factory where workers are paid very little and work many hours in very poor conditions

synthetic man-made, as opposed to made by nature

unsanitary dirty or unhealthy

upcycle to recycle something in such a way that it is made better

waterway a narrow area of water, such as a river

Further Information

Books

Plastic Planet
by Georgia Amson-Bradshaw (Franklin Watts, 2019)

This Book is Not Rubbish
by Isabel Thomas and Alex Paterson (Wren & Rook, 2018)

Reduce, Reuse, Recycle (Putting the Planet First)
by Rebecca Rissman (Wayland, 2018)

Kids Fight Plastic
by Martin Dorey and Tim Wesson (Walker Books, 2019)

Websites

www.goingzerowaste.com
www.youtube.com/channel/UCM_g2f3EWOV-OEhG7cG_Lew
Discover lots more tips from **Zero Waste Kids** author Kathryn Kellogg to continue your zero-waste journey.

https://www.overshootday.org/
Learn more about Earth overshoot day and take part in their activities.

https://nmssanctuaries.blob.core.windows.net/sanctuaries-prod/media/
archive/education/ocean_guardian/zero-waste-week/school-activities.pdf
A handy list of activities to organise a zero-waste week at school.

https://youtu.be/XzfxRUmp8eo
An informative video about the different recycling labels you find on packaging and how they can help you put packaging in the right bin.

https://youtu.be/BiSYoeqb_VY
A TED Ed video describing the lifecycle of a T-shirt.

Index

Franklin Watts
First published in Great Britain in 2020 by The Watts Publishing Group

Text copyright © Kathryn Kellogg, 2020
Design and illustration copyright © The Watts Publishing Group, 2020
All rights reserved.

Credits
Editor: Elise Short
Design: Collaborate Ltd

Every attempt has been made to clear copyright. Should there be any inadvertent omission please apply to the publisher for rectification.

HB ISBN: 978 1 4451 7111 1
PB ISBN: 978 1 4451 7112 8
eBook ISBN: 978 1 4451 7801 1

Printed in Dubai

Franklin Watts
An imprint of Hachette Children's Group
Part of The Watts Publishing Group
Carmelite House
50 Victoria Embankment
London EC4Y 0DZ

An Hachette UK Company
www.hachette.co.uk
www.franklinwatts.co.uk

FSC
www.fsc.org
MIX
Paper from responsible sources
FSC® C104740